HE *Still* WALKS ON WATER

STUDY GUIDE

Copyright © 2024 by Gary J. Lewis

Published by Arrows & Stones and Pathway Press & Resources

All rights reserved. No portion of this book may be reproduced, stored in a retrieval system, or transmitted in any form or by any means—electronic, mechanical, photocopy, recording, scanning, or other—except for brief quotations in critical reviews or articles, without prior written permission of the author.

Unless otherwise noted, all Scripture quotations are taken from the New King James Version®. Copyright © 1982 by Thomas Nelson. Used by permission. All rights reserved. | Scripture quotations marked KJV are taken from the King James Version of the Bible. Public domain. | Scripture quotations marked MSG are taken from THE MESSAGE, copyright © 1993, 1994, 1995, 1996, 2000, 2001, 2002 by Eugene H. Peterson. Used by permission of NavPress. All rights reserved. Represented by Tyndale House Publishers, Inc. | Scripture quotations marked NIV are taken from the Holy Bible, New International Version®, NIV®. Copyright © 1973, 1978, 1984, 2011 by Biblica, Inc.™ Used by permission of Zondervan. All rights reserved worldwide. www.zondervan.com. The "NIV" and "New International Version" are trademarks registered in the United States Patent and Trademark Office by Biblica, Inc.™ | Scripture quotations marked NLT are taken from the Holy Bible, New Living Translation, copyright © 1996, 2004, 2015 by Tyndale House Foundation. Used by permission of Tyndale House Publishers, Inc., Carol Stream, Illinois 60188. All rights reserved. All rights reserved.

For foreign and subsidiary rights, contact the author.

Cover design by: Sara Young
Cover photo by: Max Reyes

ISBN: 978-1-962401-49-4   1 2 3 4 5 6 7 8 9 10

Printed in the United States of America

STUDY GUIDE

HE *Still* WALKS *ON* WATER

Gary J. Lewis

ARROWS & STONES
Pathway
PRESS & RESOURCES

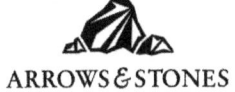

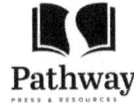

CONTENTS

CHAPTER 1. Riding into the Storm 6

CHAPTER 2. From Mountain to Valley 12

CHAPTER 3. Get in the Boat 18

CHAPTER 4. Our Intercessor 22

CHAPTER 5. God, Where Are You? 28

CHAPTER 6. Going for a Walk 34

CHAPTER 7. Light in the Darkness 40

CHAPTER 8. What's It Like to Sink? 46

CHAPTER 9. When God's in the Boat 52

CHAPTER 10. Here Comes the Son 58

CHAPTER 11. Oh, Come Let Us Adore Him ... 62

CHAPTER 12. There's a Miracle Waiting! 68

CHAPTER 1

RIDING INTO THE STORM

I don't know why bad things happen to God's people, or to anyone for that matter. But of this much, I am sure: sooner or later in life, we will all face obstacles.

READING TIME

As you read Chapter 1: "Riding into the Storm" in *He Still Walks on Water*, review, reflect on, and respond to the text by answering the following questions.

REVIEW, REFLECT, AND RESPOND

What can you learn about finding God in the middle of upheaval from the author's story about his bike accident?

_____
_____
_____
_____
_____

Think about the most difficult obstacle you have ever faced or a time when your life was turned upside down. What kind of questions did you have about God? Why?

_____
_____
_____
_____
_____

In the context of that obstacle, describe how God later revealed the purpose of your pain. How has that revelation changed the way you respond to life's storms now?

_____
_____
_____
_____
_____

> *Then Job arose, tore his robe, and shaved his head; and he fell to the ground and worshiped. And he said: "Naked I came from my mother's womb, and naked shall I return there. The LORD gave, and the LORD has taken away; blessed be the name of the LORD." In all this Job did not sin nor charge God with wrong.*
>
> —Job 1:20–22

Consider the scripture above and answer the following questions:

What elements of Job's experience, including his response to many losses, can you relate to, and which feel unfamiliar or inaccessible? Why?

_____
_____
_____
_____
_____
_____
_____
_____

The scripture says that Job "did not sin nor charge God with wrong." Why do you think Job continued to trust in God's providence, wisdom, and character?

_____
_____
_____
_____
_____
_____
_____

Make a list of all the ways Jesus has helped you through the toughest seasons of your life, and for each, identify what you learned about His heart.

_____
_____
_____
_____
_____
_____
_____
_____
_____
_____

What do you think is the relationship between our losses and the blessings that follow, if any?

_____
_____
_____
_____
_____
_____
_____
_____
_____
_____

Who would you be now if you had not faced the storms of your past? Would anything be missing? If so, what?

_____
_____
_____
_____
_____
_____
_____
_____
_____
_____

God responds to Job's doubt with a series of questions. What do these questions tell you about the sovereignty of God and His rule over your circumstances?

_____
_____
_____
_____
_____
_____
_____
_____
_____
_____

NOTES

CHAPTER 2

FROM MOUNTAIN TO VALLEY

Whether on the mountain or in the valley, we can be grateful that we don't have to face life's ups and downs in isolation.

READING TIME

As you read Chapter 2: "From Mountain to Valley" in *He Still Walks on Water*, review, reflect on, and respond to the text by answering the following questions.

REVIEW, REFLECT, AND RESPOND

Compare and contrast your relationship with God when you are in the valleys vs. the mountaintops. Provide examples.

_____
_____
_____
_____
_____
_____
_____
_____

Re-read the story about how God brought a miracle report of the author's complete recovery. What would your life look like if you entered into hopeless situations with an unwavering confidence that God would move on your behalf?

_____
_____
_____
_____
_____
_____
_____
_____

> *Suddenly, two men, Moses and Elijah, appeared and began talking with Jesus. They were glorious to see. And they were speaking about his exodus from this world, which was about to be fulfilled in Jerusalem. Peter and the others had fallen asleep. When they woke up, they saw Jesus' glory and the two men standing with him. As Moses and Elijah were starting to leave, Peter, not even knowing what he was saying, blurted out, "Master, it's wonderful for us to be here! Let's make three shelters as memorials—one for you, one for Moses, and one for Elijah."*
>
> —Luke 9:30-33 (NLT)

Consider the scripture above and answer the following questions:

How do you make sense of Peter's response to the glory of Jesus revealed and Moses and Elijah's appearance in relation to your own faith walk?

_____
_____
_____
_____
_____

The disciples fell asleep during Jesus' transfiguration. How does this symbolize our own response to Jesus when we are weary? What do you think their sudden awakening suggests about how we interact with Jesus?

_____
_____
_____
_____
_____
_____

Review the author's experience with the body of Christ during his stay at the hospital. In what ways might God's provision in the valleys be a bigger blessing than the removal of them?

_____
_____
_____
_____
_____
_____
_____
_____
_____
_____

How could you become more receptive to moving wherever Jesus takes you, even if that is into a valley?

_____
_____
_____
_____
_____
_____
_____
_____
_____
_____

How would you describe the ebb and flow of our faith walk with Jesus?

_____
_____
_____
_____
_____
_____
_____
_____
_____
_____
_____

Describe how your mountaintops prepare you for the valleys ahead, and how your valleys prepare you for upcoming mountaintops.

_____
_____
_____
_____
_____
_____
_____
_____
_____
_____
_____
_____
_____

NOTES

CHAPTER 3

GET IN THE BOAT

While we may not like the idea of rowing into the midst of chaos and disaster, we have to get in the boat.

READING TIME

As you read Chapter 3: "Get in the Boat" in He Still Walks on Water, review, reflect on, and respond to the text by answering the following questions.

REVIEW, REFLECT, AND RESPOND

In this chapter, the author encourages us to "face the storm." In your view, what does this entail?

_____
_____
_____
_____
_____

The author shares how he was able to take a less addictive route to pain management, despite the doctor's predictions. What does this tell you about facts vs. Truth?

_____
_____
_____
_____
_____

What can we learn from the story of Shadrach, Meshach, and Abed-Nego in Daniel 3:8-30 about how our storms serve as a witness to the power and glory of the Most High?

_____
_____
_____
_____
_____

> *When Jesus heard that, He said, "This sickness is not unto death, but for the glory of God, that the Son of God may be glorified through it." Now Jesus loved Martha and her sister and Lazarus. So, when He heard that he was sick, He stayed two more days in the place where He was.*
>
> —John 11:4-6

Consider the scripture above and answer the following questions:

In your own words, explain the meaning of this scripture. If you could identify one takeaway message exemplified in this passage, what would it be?

_____
_____
_____
_____
_____
_____
_____

How do you reconcile Jesus' love for Mary, Martha, and Lazarus with His response to the news of Lazarus' death?

_____
_____
_____
_____
_____
_____
_____

Recall a time when someone in your life was positively impacted by the fruit of your hardship. What did that feel like?

_____
_____
_____
_____
_____
_____

What storm are you going through right now that you are having a hard time making sense of? Write down everything you do know and the blessings of each.

_____
_____
_____
_____
_____
_____

Refer to the four things we can do to trust God's plan even when it's unclear. Create a game plan for how you can start putting each one into practice.

_____
_____
_____
_____
_____
_____

CHAPTER 4

OUR INTERCESSOR

It is a powerful ministry to pray for others and a blessing to see God work in their lives.

READING TIME

As you read Chapter 4: "Our Intercessor" in *He Still Walks on Water*, review, reflect on, and respond to the text by answering the following questions.

REVIEW, REFLECT, AND RESPOND

What does it mean to you to have Jesus as your intercessor? What pictures or images come to mind?

_____
_____
_____
_____
_____
_____
_____
_____
_____

Have you ever focused your prayers on others during a time when you needed deliverance? If so, in what ways did it comfort and sustain you?

_____
_____
_____
_____
_____
_____
_____
_____
_____

> *I urge, then, first of all, that petitions, prayers, intercession, and thanksgiving be made for all people—for kings and all those in authority, that we may live peaceful and quiet lives in all godliness and holiness.*
>
> —1 Timothy 2:1-2 (NIV)

Consider the scripture above and answer the following questions:

Timothy charges us to continually pray "for all people." List 3 people in your life who need your prayers. How might prioritizing them release you from your own burdens?

_____
_____
_____
_____
_____
_____

What do you think Timothy means when he says that our intercession will enable us to "live peaceful and quiet lives in all godliness and holiness"?

_____
_____
_____
_____
_____
_____
_____

Do you ever find yourself asking Jesus to stop the wind and waves rather than give you the courage and grace to face them? Why do you think Jesus is more concerned with the latter?

How often do you ask your main support system to pray for you? Why?

Identify a time in your life when God answered a prayer that felt like an impossible ask.

_____
_____
_____
_____
_____
_____
_____
_____
_____
_____
_____

Consider the parable in Luke 11:5-8 and explore the roles of the three friends in the story (the one with the need, the one who can meet the need, and the one who brings the two together). When in your life have you been the first friend? The second? The third?

_____
_____
_____
_____
_____
_____
_____
_____
_____
_____

NOTES

CHAPTER 5

GOD, WHERE ARE YOU?

He is always on time, even when we think He's running late.

READING TIME

As you read Chapter 5: "God, Where Are You?" in He Still Walks on Water, review, reflect on, and respond to the text by answering the following questions.

REVIEW, REFLECT, AND RESPOND

Have you ever had a powerful experience communing with God in the "fourth watch of the night" (see Matthew 14:25)? If not, why do you think this time could be so impactful?

_____
_____
_____
_____
_____
_____
_____
_____

How does the Matthew 14:25 Scripture reference illustrate the providence of God's timetable and the nearsightedness of our own?

_____
_____
_____
_____
_____
_____
_____
_____
_____

> *But do not forget this one thing, dear friends: With the Lord, a day is like a thousand years, and a thousand years are like a day. The Lord is not slow in keeping his promise, as some understand slowness. Instead, he is patient with you, not wanting anyone to perish, but everyone to come to repentance.*
>
> —2 Peter 3:8-9 (NIV)

Consider the scripture above and answer the following questions:

Does Peter's portrayal of God's timing challenge or reinforce your understanding of time in relation to God? How so? Provide a few examples.

_____
_____
_____
_____
_____
_____
_____

When have you felt that a prayer was not being answered in your timing? In what ways might the delay have been a form of protection? How is waiting relevant to repentance?

_____
_____
_____
_____
_____
_____
_____

Think about a time when you have experienced indescribable joy and peace while waiting for the Lord to answer your prayers and a time when you battled to maintain your faith. Compare and contrast those experiences. What do you attribute the differences to?

_____
_____
_____
_____
_____
_____
_____
_____
_____
_____

The author states that God is "always working behind the scenes." Explore an example of God's "behind the scenes" work in your own life.

_____
_____
_____
_____
_____
_____
_____
_____
_____

Read the short story about the author's experience at the McDonald's drive-thru with his wife. In what ways can you relate to his response to the inconvenience of waiting?

_____
_____
_____
_____
_____
_____
_____
_____
_____
_____

Describe a time when you took matters into your own hands rather than waiting on God. What was the outcome of that decision?

_____
_____
_____
_____
_____
_____
_____
_____
_____
_____

NOTES

CHAPTER 6

GOING FOR A WALK

When we can't go to Him, He comes to us. When He comes to us in our storm, He comes to us victorious over it.

READING TIME

As you read Chapter 6: "Going for a Walk" in *He Still Walks on Water*, review, reflect on, and respond to the text by answering the following questions.

REVIEW, REFLECT, AND RESPOND

The author mentions John 8:44 (NIV) in describing the works of the devil. This scripture states that he "speaks from his own resources." What do you think this means in the context of the entire verse?

_____
_____
_____
_____
_____
_____
_____
_____

Refer to the three key lessons the author learned in the early days of his accident (prayer accomplishes more than worry, Jesus hasn't changed, He is my firm foundation). Take a moment to craft your own prayers that represent each lesson.

_____
_____
_____
_____
_____
_____
_____
_____

> *We are troubled on every side, yet not distressed; we are perplexed, but not in despair; persecuted, but not forsaken; cast down, but not destroyed; always bearing about in the body the dying of the Lord Jesus, that the life also of Jesus might be made manifest in our body.*
>
> —2 Corinthians 4:8-10 (KJV)

Consider the scripture above and answer the following questions:

How do you reconcile the way Paul describes the mind of the believer made new in Christ with our feelings as we endure suffering?

_____

_____

_____

_____

_____

_____

_____

_____

In your own words, how would you describe the differences between each word pairing (e.g., perplexed vs. despair)?

_____

_____

_____

_____

_____

_____

_____

_____

What would living your life knowing that Jesus is coming towards you instead of pulling away from you during trials look like?

_____
_____
_____
_____
_____
_____
_____
_____
_____
_____

The author states that fear causes us to forget God's faithfulness in our lives. Think about a time when you doubted God's faithfulness. What were you afraid of?

_____
_____
_____
_____
_____
_____
_____
_____
_____
_____

Knowing that Jesus has given us the victory that He won, what does it mean to be victorious even when our circumstances look like the opposite?

_____
_____
_____
_____
_____
_____
_____
_____
_____

Have you ever felt God meet you in the midst of your sin, pain, fear, depression, and discouragement? What did you feel and how did you know it was Him?

_____
_____
_____
_____
_____
_____
_____
_____
_____

NOTES

CHAPTER 7

LIGHT IN THE DARKNESS

When we can't go to Him, He comes to us. When He comes to us in our storm, He comes to us victorious over it.

READING TIME

As you read Chapter 7: "Light in the Darkness" in *He Still Walks on Water*, review, reflect on, and respond to the text by answering the following questions.

REVIEW, REFLECT, AND RESPOND

Write 3 promises found in the Word of God that pertain to your present circumstances.

1. _____

2. _____

3. _____

Why did you choose those? In what ways do they bring you comfort?

_____
_____
_____
_____
_____

What did you think Jesus endured that mimics what you are experiencing now? Describe.

_____
_____
_____
_____
_____

> *Now that we know what we have—Jesus, this great High Priest with ready access to God—let's not let it slip through our fingers. We don't have a priest who is out of touch with our reality. He's been through weakness and testing, experienced it all—all but the sin. So, let's walk right up to him and get what He is so ready to give. Take the mercy, accept the help.*
>
> —Hebrews 4:14-16 (MSG)

Consider the scripture above and answer the following questions:

The author of this scripture admonishes us to "not let it slip through our fingers." How could you apply this notion of doubting Jesus in the midst of our storms as a missed opportunity?

_____
_____
_____
_____
_____
_____
_____

According to this passage, sin is the only thing that is not shared between us and Jesus. Why is that so important?

_____
_____
_____
_____
_____
_____
_____

In Matthew 14, the disciples mistook Jesus for an apparition when He appeared on the water. How has fear clouded your judgment and prevented you from seeing things as they really were? Provide an example.

_____
_____
_____
_____
_____
_____
_____
_____
_____
_____

Explore a time when God showed up in your life as I AM. What did He teach you?

_____
_____
_____
_____
_____
_____
_____
_____
_____
_____

What is the potential repercussion of asking God to deliver you quickly and change your circumstances rather than asking Him to see you through the storm?

_____
_____
_____
_____
_____
_____
_____
_____
_____

Which of Jesus' experiences with human weakness can you relate to the most? The least? How so?

_____
_____
_____
_____
_____
_____
_____
_____
_____
_____
_____

NOTES

CHAPTER 8

WHAT'S IT LIKE TO SINK?

When we allow fear to rule, it diminishes our faith. But where faith rules, it drives fear away.

READING TIME

As you read Chapter 8: "What's It Like to Sink?" in He Still Walks on Water, review, reflect on, and respond to the text by answering the following questions.

REVIEW, REFLECT, AND RESPOND

In this chapter, the author boldly declares that "we can never walk on water if we never get out of the boat." What boat is God calling you out of? Have you stepped out, and if not, why not?

_____
_____
_____
_____
_____
_____
_____

Drawing from Matthew 14, the author states that "Peter started to sink when he took his eyes off Jesus and put them on the storm." How does Peter's predicament apply to your circumstances?

_____
_____
_____
_____
_____
_____
_____

> *Do not neglect the spiritual gift you received through the prophecy spoken over you when the elders of the church laid their hands on you. Give your complete attention to these matters. Throw yourself into your tasks so that everyone will see your progress. Keep a close watch on how you live and on your teaching. Stay true to what is right for the sake of your own salvation and the salvation of those who hear you.*
>
> —1 Timothy 4:14-16 (NLT)

Consider the scripture above and answer the following questions:

What do you think this passage is saying about the importance of the body of Christ in the context of this chapter's theme—our fear and God's love?

_____
_____
_____
_____
_____
_____

Recall a time when a friend, family member, or church elder shouldered the burden of your fear... What about a time when you did the same for someone else? What was that experience like?

_____
_____
_____
_____
_____
_____
_____

What has God impressed upon your heart to do, and how could you take the first step of faith?

_____
_____
_____
_____
_____
_____
_____
_____
_____

The author describes three types of faith depicted in Matthew 14 (no faith, little faith, and great faith). Provide examples of each from your own life. What do they tell you about the evolution of your faith walk?

_____
_____
_____
_____
_____
_____
_____
_____
_____

In your own words, how would you describe the difference between man's love and God's love?

_____

_____

_____

_____

_____

_____

_____

_____

_____

_____

_____

Per Paul's description of Christ's love in Ephesians 3:17-19, what does it mean for the love of Christ to "move in all directions"?

_____

_____

_____

_____

_____

_____

_____

_____

_____

_____

_____

NOTES

CHAPTER 9

WHEN GOD'S IN THE BOAT

God's plan is bigger than our storm, and His purposes are greater than our circumstances. God will turn them around for our good and His glory.

READING TIME

As you read Chapter 9: "When God's in the Boat" in *He Still Walks on Water*, review, reflect on, and respond to the text by answering the following questions.

REVIEW, REFLECT, AND RESPOND

Where can you see God's hand at work in a past tragedy or place of pain? How do you think God used it for His greater purpose?

_____
_____
_____
_____
_____
_____
_____
_____
_____

In what ways did your relationship with God, prayer life, or general faith in Him change as a result of that?

_____
_____
_____
_____
_____
_____
_____
_____

> *But now, do not therefore be grieved or angry with yourselves because you sold me here; for God sent me before you to preserve life. For these two years, the famine has been in the land, and there are still five years in which there will be neither plowing nor harvesting. And God sent me before you to preserve a posterity for you in the earth and to save your lives by a great deliverance. So now it was not you who sent me here, but God.*
>
> —Genesis 45:5-8

Consider the scripture above and answer the following questions:

What does this passage tell you about God's sovereignty over betrayal and oppression?

_____
_____
_____
_____
_____
_____
_____

How can you apply Joseph's radical forgiveness of his brothers to your own life? How could you respond differently to tragedy and burdens in the future?

_____
_____
_____
_____
_____
_____
_____

Reflect on a time when God took your loss and pain and used it for good. Who did it impact? Explain.

_____
_____
_____
_____
_____
_____
_____
_____
_____
_____

The author recounts the tragic loss of his church's tabernacle and how God used it to knit people together. Jot down a list of all the ways God could use your calamity, loneliness, loss, or burdens for good.

_____
_____
_____
_____
_____
_____
_____
_____

Why do you think the storms of our lives happen for us and not to us? Use an example and elaborate.

_____
_____
_____
_____
_____
_____
_____
_____
_____
_____

The author warns us that Satan will come knocking when we are our most vulnerable. How could you use His lies to your advantage?

_____
_____
_____
_____
_____
_____
_____
_____
_____
_____

NOTES

CHAPTER 10

HERE COMES THE SON

The revelation of Jesus wasn't found in the miracle. It was discovered in the storm.

REVIEW, REFLECT, AND RESPOND

READING TIME

As you read Chapter 10: "Here Comes the Son" in He Still Walks on Water, review, reflect on, and respond to the text by answering the following questions.

During times of weakness, do you tend to move forward with grit and determination or shrink back and wallow? Explain.

_____
_____
_____
_____
_____

Refer to the author's story about the nurse's response to his miraculous healing. What does this tell you about our storms in the context of the bigger picture?

_____
_____
_____
_____
_____

The author cites four biblical characters (Deborah, Zechariah and Elizabeth, Moses) who displayed radical trust in challenging times. Which of the four stood out to you the most and why?

_____
_____
_____
_____
_____

> *Then He went up into the boat to them, and the wind ceased. And they were greatly amazed in themselves beyond measure and marveled. For they had not understood about the loaves, because their heart was hardened.*
>
> —Mark 6:51-52

Consider the scripture above and answer the following questions:

How does the disciples' "amazement" indicate a lack of recognition of who Jesus was?

_____
_____
_____
_____
_____
_____
_____
_____

Why do you think it is so much easier to see the storm than it is to see the blessings in the storm and God's omnipotence? Explore an example from your own life.

_____
_____
_____
_____
_____
_____
_____

Zechariah and Elizabeth remained faithful to God during the waiting for the fulfillment of His promise. What does remaining faithful in seasons of waiting look like for you?

_____
_____
_____
_____
_____
_____

How could your most tumultuous storms be a set-up for God's goodness in your life? Can you think of any personal experiences you have had with this?

_____
_____
_____
_____
_____
_____

Refer to Mark 8:17-21 in this chapter. In what ways has Jesus reminded you of His power and love for you in past trouble?

_____
_____
_____
_____
_____
_____

CHAPTER 11

OH, COME LET US ADORE HIM

It is vital to cling to the practice of worship because our storms can steal it away.

READING TIME

As you read Chapter 11: "Oh, Come Let Us Adore Him" in *He Still Walks on Water*, review, reflect on, and respond to the text by answering the following questions.

REVIEW, REFLECT, AND RESPOND

How do you endure the storms of your life, knowing that it could last months or years?

_____
_____
_____
_____
_____
_____
_____
_____
_____

Do you ever struggle to worship God when things look bleak or aren't going your way? Why do our storms seem to grow larger when disengage from worship?

_____
_____
_____
_____
_____
_____
_____
_____
_____

> *Though the fig tree may not blossom, nor fruit be on the vines; though the labor of the olive may fail, and the fields yield no food; though the flock may be cut off from the fold, and there be no herd in the stalls—yet I will rejoice in the Lord, I will joy in the God of my salvation. The Lord God is my strength; He will make my feet like deer's feet, And He will make me walk on my high hills.*
>
> —Habakkuk 3:17-19

Consider the scripture above and answer the following questions:

Can you recall a specific instance in your life when you had to rely solely on faith, without tangible evidence of deliverance? What was the end result?

_____
_____
_____
_____
_____
_____
_____

What do you think Habakkuk means by "He will make my feet like deer's *feet*, And He will make me walk on my high hills"? How can you apply this to times when you can't see an end in sight?

_____
_____
_____
_____
_____
_____
_____

What does praise and worship look like outside of church? How could you better praise Him in the midst of mundane day-to-day tasks and despite perpetual distractions?

_____
_____
_____
_____
_____
_____
_____
_____
_____
_____

What about God should we focus on when we worship? When does our "worship" become self-centered?

_____
_____
_____
_____
_____
_____
_____
_____
_____
_____

What defensive and offensive weapons do you sometimes use to ward off threats that oppose the spiritual weapons God ordained for us to wield?

_____
_____
_____
_____
_____
_____
_____
_____
_____
_____

Does or has your worship ever felt dependent on the ebbs and flows of your life? Why is God still worthy of worship even in our lowest places?

_____
_____
_____
_____
_____
_____
_____
_____
_____
_____

NOTES

CHAPTER 12

THERE'S A MIRACLE WAITING!

If we can hold and simply row a little while longer, we have God's promise of strength and victory.

READING TIME

As you read Chapter 12: "There's a Miracle Waiting!" in *He Still Walks on Water*, review, reflect on, and respond to the text by answering the following questions.

REVIEW, REFLECT, AND RESPOND

What is the danger in the adoption that all "truths" are an equally valid way to heaven? Why is it dangerous to espouse while we are here on earth?

_____
_____
_____
_____
_____
_____
_____
_____
_____

Who do you know who walks in the complete authority of Jesus' name? What kind of fruit do you see in their lives?

_____
_____
_____
_____
_____
_____
_____
_____
_____

> *For we are not fighting against flesh-and-blood enemies, but against evil rulers and authorities of the unseen world, against mighty powers in this dark world, and against evil spirits in the heavenly places.*
>
> —Ephesians 6:12 (NLT)

Consider the scripture above and answer the following questions:

If we are not in a flesh and blood battle, then how should we approach conflict?

_____
_____
_____
_____
_____
_____
_____

How are you fighting your battles and who are you fighting against? Is it serving you (in your workplace, relationships, spiritual life, etc.)? Elaborate why or why not in detail.

_____
_____
_____
_____
_____
_____
_____
_____
_____

How could you put Paul's command in 2 Corinthians 10:3-5 into practice with greater diligence?

_____
_____
_____
_____
_____
_____
_____
_____
_____
_____

Think about an area in your life where you feel stuck or frustrated. What are you expecting will happen? Do you expect Jesus to show up?

_____
_____
_____
_____
_____
_____
_____
_____
_____
_____

The author advises that when we grow weary, we simply must wait on the Lord. What are your beliefs about waiting as an active versus a passive behavior?

_____
_____
_____
_____
_____
_____
_____
_____
_____

Review the author's seven "steps to solutions" (worship, listen, believe, serve, stand, wait, and expect). What kind of changes could you make in each one of these categories to build your faith and trust in God?

_____
_____
_____
_____
_____
_____
_____
_____
_____
_____

NOTES

www.ingramcontent.com/pod-product-compliance
Lightning Source LLC
Chambersburg PA
CBHW062121080426
42734CB00012B/2941